Between the Mess and Magic

MANUSTRIUM
MEDIA

Manustrium Media
848 S Indianapolis Ave
Tulsa OK 74112

Anthology copyright 2024 Manustrium Media

Individual copyrights retained by each contributor

ISBN: 979-8-9859486-6-0 *(Paperback)*
      979-8-9859486-7-7 *(ebook)*

LCCN | 2024913062

Editor | Jes McCutchen

Cover Design | Jes McCutchen

Formatting | Racheal Daodu

Dedication

by Briana Forbes

There's something so profoundly beautiful, unmistakable, unmeasurable, and divergent about the experience of parenthood. It is all together the same but unique to each of us. We give more of ourselves than we could have ever known to take for ourselves. We grab the glimmers between globs of God knows what. We love, laugh, and cry as the pencil marked inches up the wall go by. With every story, moment, memory, and feeling shared, I felt more and more like the humanity of parenthood has a voice, a wisdom, a strength and a softness that can never be fully captured or contained.

This one's for the parents,

Bri

Contents

Dedication by Briana Forbes: iii

Ashe Eastwood | (they/them) 2
    Family Caravan 3
    Transient Lives 5
    Who Unschools Who 8
    You Called it Postpartum Madness,
    I Called It Breaking Generational Chains 10
    Complete Machine 12
    mundane bliss 14

Kid Spectral (they/them) | Bebop Blues 17
    Rapids 18
    Too Big Birthday 20
    Word Association Game 22
    Bubbles (Trapped Air) 24
    Separate 26
    Bebop Haiku 27
    Abracadeuces 28
    Stakes 29

A. Natalya Martin (they/she) 32
    They always say 33
    I hope you remember 34
    Sorry I'm an angry riser 35
    Your hands 36

Josh Wann (he/him) | Blended 38
    We Only Ever Want What's Best 39
    Parental Verbs 40

Spring Saturday 41
The Perfect Family Car 42
The Dignity of Language and Mothering 43
To the Captain's and Maymay's 44
Our Family is Like Your Favorite Starbucks Drink: Blended 45

Jes McCutchen (she/her) 47
7 48
13 50
14 51
we stand 53
3 54
5 57

Afterword: By Emily Heinz 60

About the Contributors: 64
Ashe Eastwood (they/them) 64
Kid Spectral (they/them) 65
A. Natalya Martin (she/they) 66
Josh Wann (he/him) 67
Jes McCutchen (she/her) 68
M. Torres (she/her) 69
Briana Forbes (she/her) 70
Emily Heinz (she/her) 71

Acknowledgements: 72

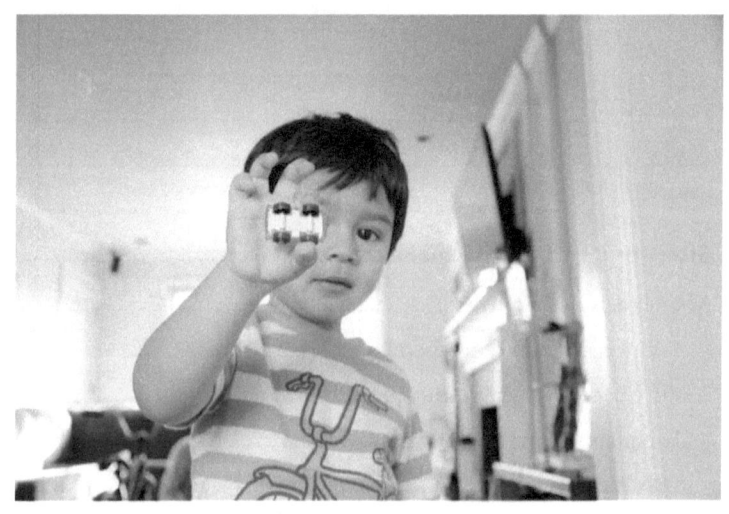

Miniature Marvel: Toddler's Delight

M. Torres

Ashe Eastwood | (they/them)

Family Caravan

Transient Lives

Who Unschools Who

You Called it Postpartum Madness,
    I Called it Breaking Generational Chains

Complete Machines

mundane bliss

Family Caravan

riding though hills
there's elves or hell
depending on you ask

maybe one in the same
but the sameness forgets to ask
either way it's a one way track

of taking care of things we're told
of taking liberties with something old
of discarding what's not yours to hold

all your things have wings
boxes filled with your childhood ease
grandma's ceramic cabbages

I'll hold you while I can
I'll hold your history
I'll hold your cabbages

but I can't promise forever
to your cabbages
even if I could give it to you

no more than I give it to everyone
except the ones we made
from two hearts and my body

there's gum stuck
under this seat
it's not that serious

this song
and Kansas
on repeat

there's
   still
      brilliance
         in
            the
               bleak

Transient Lives

I have worked on my feet
all my life
then you came through
so I worked on you

if I'm honest I was lost
like the space between suns
no idea what to do
not with me and not with you

so I learned to tie you
around my hips
your chin tucked into my spine
not for the first time

I walked you
I walked me too
over jasper sands
and red desert lands

I walked you on my back
over miles
and selenite piles
all styles of Gaia

and when freckles
began to appear on your Irish nose
I walked you here
to stand on your own

in the shadows
of the greats
perfumed like butterscotch
yellow bellied pines

to dip your toes
into a river of 7 springs
pink onion flowers
alder

and now you walk
on you own
but we still walk
together

over desert sands
canyonlands
mesa tops
log in rot

up mountain sides
down mudslides
lava domes
chipmonk homes

dragon backs
river beds
fae mounds
little mountain towns

cities deep
with folx who creep
in shadows
lined with graffiti

tags
from other lands
fill these spaces
scenery for transient lives

and to keep you
only in the forest
erases
those stories

so I take your hand
but I never ask
you to
 avert
  your
   eyes

Who Unschools Who

down in the holler
the hills bleed green
you meet a word
saturation

building dams
into dreams
encouraging their demise
purposely buildings on the river's edge

the feeling's relatable

round and round and round
stamping prints
into rich ground
hanging upside down

face on chin
comic relief
in this epic tragedy
baby, you win again and again and again

you know what we don't
its all a farse
pulling carts
like someone elses mule

you say, "I can play that game too"
mock the meetings
laugh like the monk
say, "busy busy busy"

you remember what we forgot
you are your own cart
you pave your own lot
clear as crystalline from the start

what can be done
but set you free
to be your own kind
of busy busy busy

building dams
into dreams
mud traps
you scream

"let the river in!"
with wizard arms and a wicked grin
"saturate!"
then begin again

you teach me
how to love things
for just a moment
impermanence

so I look to you
stomping about
to take my cue
drag me around in the yarrow and rue

I'll let you
for you
  are
    the
      richest
        earth

You Called it Postpartum Madness, I Called It Breaking Generational Chains

some days
on morning's brow
I'd kick the sheet back
mad and howling
like a weary wind

from above
a sad song playing
left praying
"will this ever leave me?"
"will this grief deceive me?"

will one day
I stop waking
shaking
forgetting :
I don't live in that place anymore

in my dream
your little hand
searches for mine
clinging to me
from behind

the staircase ahead is unlit
I still know it
know where it ascends
but if we take it
depends on who is waiting at the top

if no one is there
calling us up the stairs
then I don't dare
because while i've been here before
I don't live
      around
            those
                  parts
                      anymore

Complete Machine

soldering your ball
to my chain
I told you
was a low risk move

I lied

being a chain
you found me
rusted
resting
recovering

you thought
you could
forever
rest
with me

but I dragged us
to the river
used the grasses
to scrub us clean

you're welcome

I learned
so slowly
to drag your weight
as grounding and secure as it is
forward

the weight of you
I learned
could propel me
further
than I could inch myself

I was savage
you learned
that a chain
scrubbed clean and fortified
will drag a ball

this way and that
up and up and up
because even if you forget
ball were not made to rest
and chains were not made to rust

you once apologized
for our babe
said
I'm sorry
you have two balls to drag now

I said
don't be mistaken
my love
that child
understands

we
   come
      as
         complete
            machines

mundane bliss

there is nothing profound
in sudsing stains on vestibules
despite romantic words
or romantic notions
about rhythm and ritual

vinegar stinks, bubbles
in piles of soda
the alchemy isn't lost on me
I still can't unsee
what a waste of me this could be

wrists wringing, throat singing
made the task
an initiation
lit the wick, air made thick
with camphor oils

still
minutes turned minute
my voice playing mute
misaligned and resigned
end of day sighs

I really did try
but in my minds eye
devised plan after plan
to back us out of this
mundane bliss

I don't want to darn your damn socks
or fold your clothes
but I do want to love you
I just don't understand
how that's a fucking paradox

I want to hold you
for a little while
let your toes touch my toes
in the early morning before
I slip out

to climb mountains
to break walls
to swim for miles and miles and miles
until I'm free
and concluded

and then
if you'll still have me
I'll come back home
to warm my feet
by
  the
    fire
      you
        keep
          burning
            for
              me

Parenting Hack: How to instill a sense of environmental citizenship and have fun while doing it

Jes McCutchen

Kid Spectral (they/them) | Bebop Blues

    Rapids

    Too Big Birth Day

    Word Association Game

    Bubbles (Trapped Air)

    Separate

    Bebop Haiku

    Abracadeuces

    Stakes

Rapids

What is it to be in the middle of a river,
in the midst of such ravenous rapids,
clinging desperately to an ivy-covered oak,
hanging on for dear life, but in the face of the poison,
cracking jokes?
I can tell you from experience.
It's a surreal instinctual reaction that reeks of manic episode;
it's an interesting sort of rush.

I always wanted to live the sort of life that
felt like a collection of wild, nearly unbelievable stories
I could pull out of my memory and animatedly recite,
real Daniel Wallace novel type.
I can say with certainty that when I retell the story,
there's a smile on my face.
If I someday choose to tell the story to my son,
will it inspire hazardous ambitions
or give him the wrong impression?

I don't think I agree that our kids shouldn't know
who we really are or who we used to be.
Whether or not shame stains my former self-image,
I feel like it's important for him to see.
If I'm supposed to set the example,
then don't I show him self-love and acceptance
by granting those things to the entire me?

I try so hard to lead by example, and
what is it to be a parent if it isn't to lead?
A job? A title? An opportunity to observe and teach?
I like the latter the most, even if it could be all three.
I just want him to be kind and happy and just be.
I'm doing my best to show him how and check myself
simultaneously.

Self-awareness is a game changer; I just hope I can use it effectively.

This is <u>our</u> journey, after all, in all its beautiful, overwhelming, mundane glory.

Too Big Birthday

A mosaic pieced together with fragments from a million different days
is constantly shuffling in my head, certain parts replaying.

The day my son was born is fuzzy in a lot of ways.
I didn't meet him first. He was pulled from me, but I wasn't awake.
I don't think about it as a "happiest day".
It was pain-filled. It was terrifying.
It was a 'the world will never be the same'.
The good and the bad, a balancing act.
Inspiration in Themis and Atlas.
Scales of what's just, and the heavens on your back.
What is it to be a parent if it isn't to carry the world on your shoulders and
attempt to shield out the bad?

I always thought I'd die in childbirth, but I faced that day with grace and strength, I think.
I pushed for an hour, but even fully dilated, there wasn't enough space.
The room filled up as they asked how I felt about a c-section.
I wanted one anyway, so I didn't hesitate.
Then came the pain that I wasn't supposed to feel.
The meds were meant to block all that out, but here it is,
very abruptly and very intense. I threw up first then.

A group in scrubs rushed me through hallways, calling orders I didn't understand.
I was lost in the haze of the nausea and pain.
I remember my partner looked scared as he was handed scrubs and I was carted away.
I wanted to tell him I love him, and it'll be okay, but I can't find the focus to speak.

We made it to the OR, and I puked a couple more times.
They pinched me and asked if I could feel it. I told them I could and that it hurt.
They tried that a couple more times, but we were running out of time and
couldn't wait for the pain meds to work.
I remember they strapped down my arms, outstretched at my sides.
They gave me a mask and had questions to ask, but I was already checked out.
That medicine worked too fast. I went under. Everything went black.

I woke up a couple hours later in a room alone with a nurse.
I asked if my partner was okay. He hadn't been able to be in there with me after all.
I knew he'd be upset about that.
She said he was alright, and the baby was doing fine.
Now that I was awake, I could go back to my room and meet him.
It was finally time.

Word Association Game

Word association game: parent.
Is the word association game viewed differently if you often think in pictures or flashes of memories?

Parent. Remember that poem you wrote when you were fifteen about your parasites, I mean, parents? I don't remember the poem exactly, but I do recall that it had a descending list, a countdown of sorts. Maybe I knew then that it was the feeling of a ticking clock, a timebomb.
I wonder if the explosion of zero was enough force to crash through my amniotic sack and pull the life out of my uterus.

Parenting. Face to face with the culmination of a trail of thoughts and phrases,
hushed whispers nuzzled in a warm chest.
Years of passion and smiles crashing and thrashing around finally falling into place.

Parent. Pressure and expectation. A simple disregard for your feelings, needs, or wants.
Parent. Bitterness at all the crushed dreams and childish fantasies.
You know most people need a place to point the blame, and kids are an easy target.
Easier if they're taught not to complain.
People make jokes. It's even a known trope: "marriage and family are the worst,
the old ball and chain, anything to cope!" It's amusing to me to observe and note.
I've been a parent to many over my entire life, but
this time it was my choice. This time, it's mine.

Word association game: parenting.
Parent. Worlds of difference there, like a whole other plane.
Parenting and parent are nowhere near the same to me.
One is rewarding and joyful, and one is bitterness and loss of faith.
Parenting. Perspective is everything.
Parent. Trauma and pain.

I still have to separate the two concepts in my mind because I'm not ready to see parents as 'the good guys'. I'm working on healing though, and
healing takes time.

Bubbles (Trapped Air)

We're going to get through this together
because we can figure out anything together.
That's what I tell you all the time.
I hope you don't notice how very little I must seem to know.

We don't get out much yet, but
I'm trying to get us out and around others more.
I always have a million reasons to leave the blinds closed and
the doors locked.
We can stay inside where it's not so hot,
where we can play at peace,
where it's safer.

I know I can't protect you from the world, but
I can teach you how to be kind and caring.
I can teach you that you're magic too
that your words and voice matter.

We can venture through the maze of tangled emotions and
healthy growth.
Hand in hand, we'll learn how to be present and honest and
open, and
we'll learn how to speak up.

There are days that I worry
I'm all too happy to stay locked inside our bubble for longer
than we should, but
playing and existing with you is such a happy space.

Your face is full of wonder, decorated with smiles and dimpled cheeks.
You light up as you give your bravest, fiercest roar.
I don't let you dangle on the edge of your seat long.
I roar back, fierce and full, and you're delirious with laughter again.

I hope I always remember to roar with you.
I want to show you what it looks like to roar in the face of danger, and
show the world the strength that softness provides.
Maybe we can stay inside our bubble one more day.

Separate

Separation. Don't forget.
He is a tiny human.
Don't let your anxieties seep out of the lines and spill onto him.
Don't let your traumas or the way you were raised and conditioned leak out.
Separate. Don't forget.

Even on the hardest days,
when the sky's grays flood into the house
like a villainous wave,
he greets the day with smiles
and laughter filled with sunrays.
I might be filled with magic, but he has got it in spades!
My good morning boy can thaw the day's coldest frozen heart cage.

I am so lucky,
I think to myself as he greets me with a delighted squeal and a grin.
I am so lucky that I get to be here and be present.
I'm so lucky that I get to know him.

He teaches such patience; one he has never known himself.
I find the beautiful ironic humor in the mundane life we live, once again.

I am so lucky in so many ways.
I just hope that's enough
to keep me grounded and keep me sane.
Just remember to breathe deep.
Breathe deep,
and separate.

Bebop Haiku

Good morning, sweetheart
You greet the day with such light
Inspiring magic

Abracadeuces

For the first time,
I watched my son stand
from squatting beside me,
to find a freshly fallen log on the floor.
I see a bit on his foot,
as he turns to examine what he's left.

I swiftly scoop him up in all his bare-butt-baby glory
and head to his room\.

I've had dogs my entire adult life.
I'm no stranger to scrubbing excrement
from all sorts of surfaces,
but this is a first for me.

I can't help but laugh\.
I'm not surprised, but
I'm definitely tickled.

This kid looked like he was dropping the hottest album of the year,
and dropped a deuce instead.

The clean-up isn't ideal. Still,
I can't help but feel like this is the life.

These stories could build an empire.
I hope they do.
My guy could be prince of the poop tales,
king of hilarity.
The embodiment of a million reasons
to smile, grow, laugh, and shine.

Stakes

Clapping. Squealing. Roaring.

Endlessly.

This is joy.
Unfiltered.
Untainted.
Pure joy in all its totality.
This kid is profoundly gleeful.

I wonder if the duality of his joy and my melancholy is
noticeable.
I think I'm upbeat and mirthful as well,
but only in our bubble
here at home that I've created.

It feels like when the children make a sanctuary
their first night in Count Olaf's dwelling.
That's what I've done.

I'm jovial as the jester in our guarded abode, but
the outside mercilessly creeps in
through the hairline fractures and cracks.
The world doesn't feel safe anymore,
if it ever really did.

I'm good at surviving, but
I'm trying to teach how to flourish and thrive.
I can show him how to regulate and cope, but
that shouldn't be the lesson
when your environment is systematically broken.

I always say perspective is everything, so
maybe that's the key.
If I can't fix our society,
maybe I can change the way we interact with it.

Perspective shift: maybe
if the dark can creep in,
that means the light can also break through,
break out.

Maybe we can change the darker corners of the globe
by existing in our own authentic light.

We can shine our brilliance wherever we go,
in all that we do.
I bet we'll find that
that's how you let the sunshine
into a dark room.

Be a light in darkness, but
don't forget to find the light out there too.

Remember your deep breaths.
Want to do some with me?

Breathe in.

Breathe out.

Do you feel a little better?
I do too.

The 9th Ride of the Day, Red Flag

M. Torres

A. Natalya Martin (they/she)

Untitled : *They always say*

Untitled : *I hope you remember*

Untitled: *Sorry I'm an angry riser*

Untitled: *Your hands*

They always say

No rain
No flowers,
But flower can't grow
In a flood

I hope you remember

All the hide n seek
The tickle fights.
Not the mornings
When I woke up grumpy.

I hope you remember
I've cream for breakfast,
And movies past your bedtime,
Not the times I yelled,
"Hurry up!"

I hope you remember
Playgrounds,
And beach days,
And too much candy.

I hope you remember
Lullabies,
And bedtime stories,
And every sweet hug.

I hope the sad things
Roll off,
And the hard times
Fade away.

I hope you remember
The good days.

Sorry I'm an angry riser

That I greet you in the mornings
with groans instead of love.
I'm always glad to see you,
and your happy smiling face.
My soul just needs a beat
to crawl back in my body,
and shake off the night.
I promise I'll be nicer
after breakfast.

Your hands

Are so little
They could reach
Through my ribs
And hold my heart
While you fall asleep

The Funny Thing
Jes McCutchen

Josh Wann (he/him) | Blended

We Only Ever Want What's Best

Parental Verbs

Spring Saturday

The Perfect Family Car

The Dignity of Language and Mothering

To the Captain's and Maymay's

Our Family is Like Your Favorite Starbucks Drink: Blended

We Only Ever Want What's Best

We run around- us, parents-
Frantic on forms
Gluttons for guidance

Taking turns judging each other
Harshly
In our heads, to our partners,
our other parenting groups:

"Did you see what they had the kids doing?"
When we know full well we are one incident away from
A lot of explaining ourselves

We do all this in the name of
finding, making, curating the best
For our children

But my best plans can't beat
a hike in the rain
Or simply shaking hands with the ocean
or a sunset.

Those moments in nature
We don't have to blog ad nauseam or
Over "expert analysis" about it

My four year old's giggle at
the Atlantic surf is all the opinion I need-
She calls it "soda"

Parental Verbs

I fold laundry, she folds bills
I cut the chicken, she cuts rug

She folds egg into batter, I fold a sheet wrong
She cuts up with the kids, I cut the cheese

We trade these verbs around as freely as our roles,
    Expected and otherwise

These verbs make us parents
The way we use them makes us partners

Spring Saturday

We will pack books
We will pick the perfect spot
By the water
For our children to play

And not read a word
And spend the whole

Time worrying and checking
On the kids

In this way-
Our fun in bloom

The Perfect Family Car

Enough space for your kids and their extra elbows
Enough space for your luggage and plan B's

The cupholder-the perfect size for your coffee
And magically self-cleaning so there is never
That filthy little landfill of bits and loose change
At the bottom

The interior- sound proof to cut down
On city noise
And hide your screams in the garage at night

The Dignity of Language and Mothering

I recently learned that
There is an area of
A mother's stomach
-Post birth- that is called
A "mother's apron"

Just sit with it

Who came up with that?
Who noticed?
It's not enough
Mothers carry us, grow us up, and bare the evidence of all of it
up and down their bodies, their beautiful faces, and in their
ever increasing nervous dispositions

Go ahead and call this poem pandering but you find no lies
here
They must endure a pay gap and philistine policies
that not only toss them aside but tumble them
And now a cringy-anatomical nickname for the badge of
bearing life?
It's almost as bad as enduring a poem about it
from a dad

To the Captain's and Maymay's

There will be days when their bio parent break
their hearts
And you will want
to
Break
Something

You will have to pray, pace, deadlift
in quiet attic silence
annoy several sponsors and therapists with it

But the best thing your hands can do
is not breaking or pointing
or even lifting
It's holding: the parent, the kid
-yourself-
with love

Return to this over and over again
like waves touching shore
I'm here
        I'm here
        I'm here
        for you.

Our Family is Like Your Favorite Starbucks Drink: Blended

Some of mine, some of my lady's
And a garnish of us
In the form of our youngest

Being a bonus parent, having bonus kids
Means you are always clarifying
Until you're tired of explaining
and you just have to say: love.
Love love love love love love
Love love love love love love
Twins?
No, love
How are they 45 days apart?
Love
How is he robin auburn and the girls a sandy east coast sunset?
Love
Are they real sisters?
Fool, this will get you cut.
Why don't you pick on one in front of the other and find out
I love our loyal little litter that maxes out any minivan or SUV

The bureaucrats will have to keep filling out the extra
Paperwork to allow my partner and I permission
into their lives at various governmental intersections
But my heart knows
Holy Ghost Knows
what any parent knows
Names are held with hyphens
But hearts are held with hands
and a magic not captured
By really any poem much less a mark
A form
A blood

Alone with the Train

M. Torres

Jes McCutchen (she/her)

7 - i should chop you up

13 - He spoke before one

14 - Round earth mother energy

Unnumbered - *We stand*

3 - Because we value education in our family

5 - Skin itching and slightly off center

7

i should chop you up
he screams
like the mad witch in a forest
whose errand i failed
but i need her chicken leg home
for shelter

he swings the prop ax
that we bought
long ago
as part of an extensive inside joke
wielding it
like the long awaited Norse prince
come to conquer lands

can a child raised
behind a picket fence
in a suburb
where there's a Burger King
within smelling distance
(depending on the wind direction)
be considered feral?

because again he's naked
coming at me with a plastic dagger
and it's a good thing for me
that he's tiny

why are his clothes off?
why are they in the full bath tub?
why do none of his twenty pairs of shoes fit?
They're all the left one anyway

with eyeshadow i bought at CVS
he paints his cheeks
in bold red stripes
asks me to add a flame
on his forehead
slips on a wizard's cloak
elbows his way out the back door

13

he spoke before one
and at two
stopping to look
at the dead cricket
wing broken
in the entryway
of our home

he asked
"dead?"

to which I answered
"yes."

he thinks for a moment
chubby cheeks
rosy from sleep
squatting
for a closer look
cloth diaper and tshirt
cozy from his nap
finger dimples point
at the insect

then states
"it didn't wear a mask."
and toddles to his snack

14

round earth mother energy
swollen venus goddess
orb brimming with life
glowing sphere of nature's bounty

until the surgeon scooped it out
melon baller gutted
the moon once full
made crescent
yanked life
a concave vacancy

hollowed and weak
unable to move
as they choose
which bits to stuff back in
guessing where they
should probably go

the life is plump and swollen
red cheeks fierce and interesting
but he is swept away
down river to another
less hollowed bed
that waxing gibbous
more than half of me
to start our separate lives

and i lay unmoving
a log on the side of the river
what should have taken nature ions
to smooth out
to crater
to erode

takes mere blinks
and I have been emptied

then stuffed back together
meant to hold my insides
from coming back out
with a bandage and someone
else's blood

we stand

arms clasped behind our backs
poised
grim and somber

the plastic penguin is filled
with flowers I remembered to get
from Trader Joe's

and tonight is the last
the final
the thank god its over why did we have to clean that plastic shit bucket out for so long we're not servants in a medieval monastery we have indoor plumbing and two yes two whole ass working toilets in this house and yet this plastic garbage penguin we got for twelve dollars at Target is the only thing he could possibly shit in for the past two years where he's essentially be potty trained but has just refused to use the actual plumbing in this house.

but it's over
and i wrote a eulogy
to the penguin potty
and he cries
his big boy underwear casting shadows
in the candle light
because of course i lit candles
and we say goodbye

and the next day
he shits in the toilet
like we fucking knew he could

3

because we value education in our family
i state calmly.
for the fifth time.
and it's raining
because of course it's raining
and he's refusing to go into school

we want you to learn and grow
because we value education
I try to remember
I'm sick he says
your teacher will let us know if you get sick
you're safe here

i shush the gun toting right winger demon on my shoulder
whispering *liar*
and the angel on the left whispers *thoughts and prayers thoughts and prayers* on repeat
liar liar *liars*

rain has mostly stopped but we're past
the indicated drop off time

and now he has to poop
he screams that he has to poop
he cries
that he has to poop

and it has to be
at home.

and only at home.

make a u-turn take a breath
park at home
step out, take a breath
flex my hands
shake them twice and clench my fists
breath again

let him out and he runs in
to poop

at home.

and only at home.

I want to call it.
the whole rainy day has been derailed
by defecation and intrusive thoughts
and snotty muffin tears
let's just stay in bed and adhd wins
with anxiety coming in a close second
because only failures get their kids to school
tardy.

and since I've already failed
may as well just put on a pair of sweats
text my partner to call him in sick
one tally for the other team

but i load him up
drive back the way we came
check in at the front office
walk him crying to his classroom

the teacher's daughter who believes five minutes early is ten
minutes late on my right shoulder whispering *failure*
a the therapist muppet on my left whispers *imposter*

i turn away before the syndrome part rings out

then shake and cry in my car
because we value education in this family

5

Skin itching and slightly off center
Eight months postpartum
My FOXFIRE gang of employed
Adults skipped the stick-and-poke
booked professionals

Got matching flame tattoos
Sketched by Joyce Carol Oates
A surprise for Josh's birthday

I think we'd all forgotten
This coming of age novel
Was about remembering those who formed us
Who we've drifted or ripped or broken from
To become our now selves

It's hard to come of age without change
And isn't that what fire is?
Flaring up burning out
Permanent scars to wood and metal
Branches to ashes
Peeling burns that heal
Skin forever transformed
A tattoo

Subtle fade of lines
Getting together for drinks
Less often
And to catch up instead
Like records skipping

With daughters and jobs
Rebellion now is softer
The violent love of friendship in youth
Smoothed out
Harsh black lines
spread to subtle blue

We move away
Forget to write
But always the scar
The black path of trust
Midnight magic and shared stories
Mark us as each others

There will never be a last reminder
Because isn't that how blood oaths
Always work
I plan to come of age
Six or seven times

Catch glimpses
All our lives
Reflection in the bathroom mirror
Stretching on the yoga mat
Questioned by our children

Genetic Match

Jes McCutchen

Afterword: By Emily Heinz

One year, five months. Four doctors. Ovulation strips. Pregnancy tests. Tracking. Temperature taking. Vitamins, supplements, organic food. Acupuncture. Blood tests and semen analysis. Next on the docket is a laparoscopy for me and a urologist for him.

In the early days of our relationship, we daydreamed. We discussed every experience through the lens of our future, our children, our family. Once, I came home to find our dog Rosie had had explosive diarrhea in her kennel thanks to a bout of giardia. I was panicking, but he calmly talked us through the steps, "You give Rosie a bath and I'll clean this up." Afterwards, we laughed together and joked that we had seen glimpses of our future selves - I'll wash the sick baby while he washes the carpet, the clothing, the bedding.

We don't daydream much anymore. We avoid discussion of what to do with the growing piles in a junk room that was supposed to be the nursery. No longer do we fantasize about the pancake shapes we'll make on Sunday mornings, or who will pack the lunches. There wasn't a conversation or agreement about it. One day the dreaming just… stopped.

"There's still brilliance in the bleak." This line from *Family Caravan* resonated with me as a snapshot of this anthology and life as a parent. Enduring infertility has made everything less brilliant. With each passing month and failed attempt at conception, the sparkle and excitement that life once held has dimmed. Cuddling our dog between us in bed reminds me I'd rather be cuddling our baby. Weeknights when we watch Netflix after dinner, I'm reminded that I'd rather be doing bath time and bedtime stories.

Our bleak does not feel brilliant. We're living in a grayscale version of the life we imagined together.

In *Transient Lives,* Ashe Eastwood describes the adventures that I yearn for. Four years ago on a trip to Washington D.C. with my dad, I helped a little boy read about the blacksmith shop at Mount Vernon. I pointed to the anvil and forge while I read from the exhibit placard, and his eyes widened with wonder. As we exited the building, my dad said through a smile, "Everything's a lot more exciting when you get to do it with your kids." I know.

For years, I planned my life around becoming a mother. I chose a career that revolves around children. I chose a partner based on the dream that he would one day father my children. I held tightly to the idea that when I became pregnant and gave birth, my children would bring me all the wonderment, joy, and adventure I could ever need in life. I knew that I would intentionally create magical moments and experiences for my children, but now that we're here, without them, I no longer remember how to create those things for myself. Or maybe I don't want to because each occasion only serves as a painful reminder of what we don't yet have.

It feels easier to hide ourselves away from life while we wait for it to begin. We pass the time by staring at big screens and little screens and convincing ourselves we're just "homebodies." Kid Spectral's juxtaposition of home and the outside world in *Stakes* reminded me of the painful irony that I no longer feel at peace in the sanctuary of my own home. As newlyweds, we bought this house to start our family in, but now it's just an empty shell waiting to be filled with little bodies and laughter and toys. Looking around each room, I am swallowed by the enormity and the silence. My heart feels less hurt outside the walls of my home. It's lonely here.

Another painful irony - how challenging it sometimes is to be around people I love. At Foxfire brunch, where the shared stories now revolve around parenting, I have nothing to contribute. In Jes McCutchen's poem *Foxfire* she writes the lines "Getting together for drinks / Less often / And to catch up instead / Like records skipping". So I listen, retreat, and burrow deeper into myself for protection. I love my little sister and her new baby from the safety of arm's length. I host baby showers for family and coworkers because I'm the party planner. I watch the bellies of my family and friends swell, read the birth stories on insta and try my best to check in.

In *Word Association Game,* Kid Spectral highlights the duality of the word parent. During my quest to become a parent, I've also had to confront how my parents have impacted me. My mother's approach to parenting me through meltdowns sounded like this - "Emily, we don't have time for this today, we have things on our agenda so get yourself together." Now that I'm an adult, she often brags about how effective and superior her methods were since they didn't include spanking, but due to her conditioning I rarely allow myself to fully feel my emotions. It has taken years of therapy, journaling, yoga, and reflection to unlearn the harmful patterns I inherited from both her and my father.

When I started acupuncture treatments for fertility, my acupuncturist began targeting the stress that was camped out in my body. One day, she placed a needle in the muscle between my thumb and pointer finger, unleashing a wave of uncontrollable sobbing. She patted my arm, instructed me not to hold it back, and left the room.

As mild electric currents pulsed through needles into my body, I endured wave after wave of panic and fear. *Will I ever get to experience being pregnant? Will I get to experience childbirth? What if we can't have kids? What have I done to be barred from it all? What will my life be if it isn't raising babies? Why me? Why me? Why me?*

My body was convulsing, sobs erupting from my throat, and I began to worry that if I didn't calm myself down some of those needles would become dislodged. I tried a technique that I'd seen a counselor present in an Instagram reel, Radical Acceptance, or something like that. In my mind, I embraced the fear and said to myself, "I embrace this fear, this fear is a part of me, it is welcome here." My breathing slowed, my body stilled, and I was able to think more clearly about why I am afraid.

I'm afraid because I am not in control. Regardless of the work I put into researching, changing our diet and lifestyle, requesting tests from the doctor, and searching for answers, we still don't know which path to take forward.

I desperately need someone, anyone, to just tell me what to do and I will do it. I'm afraid because we have seen numerous doctors, and none of them seem to understand the urgency we feel. I'm afraid that I will never get to look at my husband as we hold our baby for the first time and feel my heart grow three sizes like the Grinch. I'm afraid we won't get any of the firsts that come with raising children.

I know that parenting comes with exhaustion, sacrifice, and pain. The pain of this journey started as a gut punch that came with my period each month, but it has turned into an aching black hole of grief and longing. I would give anything to be on the other side.

About the Contributors:

Ashe Eastwood (they/them)

Ashe Eastwood is a work from home Web Developer. After 12 years as an educator, and being radicalized by that experience, they left to focus on providing rich educational experiences to their child and community. They also run an Explorer's club in the Jemez Mountains that focuses on teaching children to enjoy and care for natural spaces. They live there with their partner and 6 year old wildling. In their spare time, they process the complexities of life, with poetry.

Kid Spectral (they/them)

Kid Spectral (they/them) is a writer, general artist, and maker. They grew up in Nashville and try their best to keep the rhythm in their step always. They currently reside in Tulsa with their partner Trey, and their son, as well as a sassy omniscient being, Meade the Dog (13 years old) and her grand-pup Albert Freedom-fighter, Alby Free for short (7 years old). They're a full-time parent who loves adventure, cartoons, and every library they've ever met. They're neurodivergent, queer, and a huge advocate for mental health and the benefits of therapy. They're always happy to connect community with resources and each other.

@kidspectralcreates on IG and kidspectralcreates@gmail.com

A. Natalya Martin (she/they)

A. Natalya Martin is the parent of one darling kid. They are an avid SFF reader, when the time to read is there, but honestly who has the time? The past year has been one of big transitions. Times are changing, and it's gonna work out. You can find her at @heartofareader on Instagram.

Josh Wann (he/him)

Josh Wann is a writer, comedian, and educator in Tulsa, OK. He has experimented and published in a variety of forms, because these prose ain't loyal. His work and performances have been featured at Studio 308, Living Arts of Tulsa, Arts @302, Oklahoma City University, Magic City Books, Tulsa Community College, The Gathering Place Tulsa, LowDown, and various other stages and publications. He gravitates towards laughter, nature, and big plates of breakfast foods with his partner/champion Amanda and a tender, raucous hoard of 4 children. He is available for custom words and events at homegrownpoet918@gmail.com or on Instagram @homegrownpoems918.

Jes McCutchen (she/her)

Jes McCutchen (she/her/hers) lives in Tulsa with her partner Marshall, and their son. As well as two completely stinky weenie dogs she loves dearly. When not writing poetry, she writes queer YA science fiction and fantasy novels that always have happy endings. She struggled with postpartum depression and anxiety, and is currently medicated and in monthly therapy. Jes is also part of a women-run small press in Tulsa, Horns & Rattles Press which specializes in short genre fiction. You can find more information and contact her at jesmccutchenwrites.com.

M. Torres (she/her)

M.Torres is a professional photographer and entrepreneur based in Tulsa, Oklahoma. With a keen eye for detail and a passion for storytelling, she specializes in capturing the beauty and essence of her subjects, whether in fine art, commercial, or portrait photography. Megan is the founder of Torres Fine Art Photography Studios and Torres & Co., where she has helped numerous small businesses grow through her marketing expertise and creative vision. She is also the acting director of a nonprofit Latin American dance group, showcasing her dedication to the arts and community. A registered photographer since 2014, Megan is known for her adaptability, hard work, and commitment to excellence. As an independent mother, she balances her career with a drive to support other businesses in finding their voice and success.

Briana Forbes (she/her)

Briana Forbes is a Weirdo, Autism Mom, B²Weird Bookclub founder and music festival enthusiast who is passionate about diversity in literature. She lives in California and minds her business.

Emily Heinz (she/her)

Emily Heinz (she/her) is an educator by trade and full time lover of dogs, nature, and her large family. She has taught at every level of public education in Oklahoma and works as a teaching coach. She and her partner Kyle, have been TTC (trying to conceive) and her contribution to the collection is the perspective from someone who is not on the other side of parenting, yet.

Acknowledgements

My forever thanks to all of the contributors to this collection who poured out some of their most intimate feelings for this book. I appreciate every single one of you, and the patience you've had as I pulled all of this together. Art takes courage. And you have all been so very brave.

And to my little dude. I hope you understand. I think you will. You're pretty clever.

Love,
Jes

www.ingramcontent.com/pod-product-compliance
Lightning Source LLC
Chambersburg PA
CBHW020234170426
43201CB00007B/427